author **Jacqueline Wilson**, taught in drama schools and written for the Stephen Joseph Theatre, Scarborough.

International work directing plays, lecturing on children's theatre and running drama workshops has taken her to many countries including Russia, the Philippines, the United Arab Emirates, Japan, Brazil, Peru, Singapore, Cyprus, Finland and Israel. In 2002, she was awarded an MBE for services to children's drama, the first of

Other Plays for Young People to Perform from Nick Hern Books

Original Plays

13
Mike Bartlett

100
Christopher Heimann,
Neil Monaghan, Diene Petterle

BLOOD AND ICE
Liz Lochhead

BOYS
Ella Hickson

BUNNY
Jack Thorne

BURYING YOUR BROTHER IN THE
  PAVEMENT
Jack Thorne

CHRISTMAS IS MILES AWAY
Chloë Moss

COCKROACH
Sam Holcroft

DISCO PIGS
Enda Walsh

EARTHQUAKES IN LONDON
Mike Bartlett

EIGHT
Ella Hickson

GIRLS LIKE THAT
Evan Placey

HOW TO DISAPPEAR COMPLETELY
  AND NEVER BE FOUND
Fin Kennedy

I CAUGHT CRABS IN WALBERSWICK
Joel Horwood

KINDERTRANSPORT
Diane Samuels

MOGADISHU
Vivienne Franzmann

MOTH
Declan Greene

THE MYSTAE
Nick Whitby

OVERSPILL
Ali Taylor

PRONOUN
Evan Placey

SAME
Deborah Bruce

THERE IS A WAR
Tom Basden

THE URBAN GIRL'S GUIDE TO
  CAMPING AND OTHER PLAYS
Fin Kennedy

THE WARDROBE
Sam Holcroft

Adaptations

ANIMAL FARM
Ian Wooldridge
Adapted from George Orwell

ARABIAN NIGHTS
Dominic Cooke

BEAUTY AND THE BEAST
Laurence Boswell

CORAM BOY
Helen Edmundson
Adapted from Jamila Gavin

DAVID COPPERFIELD
Alastair Cording
Adapted from Charles Dickens

GREAT EXPECTATIONS
Nick Ormerod and Declan Donnellan
Adapted from Charles Dickens

HIS DARK MATERIALS
Nicholas Wright
Adapted from Philip Pullman

THE JUNGLE BOOK
Stuart Paterson
Adapted from Rudyard Kipling

KENSUKE'S KINGDOM
Stuart Paterson
Adapted from Michael Morpurgo

KES
Lawrence Till
Adapted from Barry Hines

THE LOTTIE PROJECT
Vicky Ireland
Adapted from Jacqueline Wilson

MIDNIGHT
Vicky Ireland
Adapted from Jacqueline Wilson

NOUGHTS & CROSSES
Dominic Cooke
Adapted from Malorie Blackman

THE RAILWAY CHILDREN
Mike Kenny
Adapted from E. Nesbit

SWALLOWS AND AMAZONS
Helen Edmundson and Neil Hannon
Adapted from Arthur Ransome

TO SIR, WITH LOVE
Ayub Khan-Din
Adapted from E.R Braithwaite

TREASURE ISLAND
Stuart Paterson
Adapted from Robert Louis Stevenson

WENDY & PETER PAN
Ella Hickson
Adapted from J.M. Barrie

THE WOLVES OF WILLOUGHBY
  CHASE
Russ Tunney
Adapted from Joan Aiken

For more information on plays to perform visit
www.nickhernbooks.co.uk/plays-to-perform

Jacqueline Wilson

BAD GIRLS

adapted for the stage by

VICKY IRELAND

introduced by

JACQUELINE WILSON

NICK HERN BOOKS
London
www.nickhernbooks.co.uk

A Nick Hern Book

Bad Girls first published in Great Britain as a paperback original in 2006 by Nick Hern Books Limited, The Glasshouse, 49a Goldhawk Road, London W12 8QP

Reprinted 2007, 2008, 2009, 2014

Adaptation and Production Notes © 2006 Vicky Ireland
Introduction © 2006 Jacqueline Wilson

Adapted from the book by Jacqueline Wilson © 1996
First published by Doubleday in 1996

Vicky Ireland and Jacqueline Wilson have asserted their right to be identified as the authors of this work

Cover illustration © 1996, 2006 Nick Sharratt
Cover designed by Ned Hoste, 2H

Typeset by Nick Hern Books, London
Printed in Great Britain by Mimeo Ltd, Cambridgeshire PE29 6XX

A CIP catalogue record for this book is available from the British Library

ISBN   978 1 85459 910 0

Woodland
CARBON
www.woodlandcarbon.co.uk
NICK HERN BOOKS
Printed on Carbon Captured paper

INTRODUCTION

I was thrilled when Vicky Ireland got in touch with me and
said she wanted to adapt one of my books for the stage.
I immediately warmed to this pocket-sized, dynamic blonde
woman. I knew she had a brilliant track record. I knew she
understood drama. I knew she had great respect for her child
audiences. But when she said she wanted to turn *The Lottie
Project* into a play, I thought she was completely bananas. It's
a book with a split text, mostly present day, but important parts
are Victorian. There are any number of characters, lots of
school scenes, street scenes, a seaside setting, a police search
including a helicopter, and a huge amusement theme park.
How on earth could Vicky conjure this up on stage with a very
limited budget and a cast of six?

Well, *I* was the banana. She used her imagination, very clever
special effects, evocative music, a brilliant set like a large book
and a fantastic cast of actors. I'll never forget that magical first
night, sitting amongst so many spellbound children, seeing my
imaginary world become a reality on stage.

Since then, Vicky's adapted a handful of my books for the
stage. I hope she works her special magic on many more to
come! For *Bad Girls*, she picked up on the rainbow theme very
effectively. She did some research to find out school tactics
about bullying, and incorporated them in a sensitive way into
the end of the play.

Midnight presented even more of a challenge with its dark
fairy theme, but Vicky realised immediately that the actors
could work simple rod puppets for any fairy scenes, and
commissioned the most beautiful, haunting music for the fairy
dances.

I hope you will enjoy taking part in these plays and working
your own magic with them.

JACQUELINE WILSON

PRODUCTION NOTES

Principal Characters

MANDY WHITE, *eleven, a small girl, with blonde plaits and glasses. She is a shy, bullied child with an overprotective mother. Her strong imagination sometimes makes situations worse and sometimes helps her to cope with them.*

MORAG WHITE, *fifty-five, a dowdy, fussy, middle-class older mum who adores and overprotects her only daughter, Mandy.*

TOM WHITE, *sixty-two, a quiet man who enjoys painting as a hobby. Also adores Mandy, but keen to let her grow up.*

TANYA, *fourteen, a small, skinny girl with spiky orange hair. She is a feisty, cheerful, funny girl who wins hearts. She also has a sensitive side which she bottles up. An amoral fostered child.*

KIM MATTHEWS, *twelve, a tall, pretty, clever girl who uses her superior gifts to bully Mandy.*

ARTHUR KING, *eleven, a small, lonely, bespectacled boy who loves stories of chivalry.*

SARAH NEWMAN, *schoolgirl in Kim's gang.*

MRS EDWARDS, *head teacher.*

MELANIE HOLDER, *Mandy's ex-best friend, now in Kim's gang.*

MR MOSELEY, *class teacher.*

Scenes (and corresponding colours of the rainbow)

ACT ONE

Scene One   RED

Bus stop

Scene Two   ORANGE

Bus stop
Hospital
Home

Scene Three   YELLOW

Home

Scene Four   GREEN

Playground
School
Street

Scene Five   BLUE

Home
School
Department store
Swimming pool

ACT TWO

Scene Six   INDIGO

Shopping centre
Home
Tanya's house
Shopping centre
Lift
Indigo shop

Scene Seven   VIOLET

Lift
Indigo shop
Police station
Home
Tanya's house

Scene Eight   RAINBOW

Home
Library
School
Bus stop

Casting and Doubling

Bad Girls was originally performed by a cast of six adult actors, with the following doubling:

Mandy White
Morag White / Sarah Newman / Security Guard
Tom White / Bus Driver / Mrs Edwards / Policeman
Tanya / Melanie Holder / Woman in Street / Nurse
Kim Matthews / Paramedic / Policewoman / Librarian
Arthur King / Indigo Shop Assistant / Sergeant Stockton

With no doubling and large numbers of extras, the cast could be as large as required.

Set Design

The chapters in Jacqueline Wilson's novel are named after the colours of the rainbow and all contain words, emotions and objects that reflect each colour.

In the original production, the set echoed this rainbow theme and structure of the novel, with a feeling of thunder, rain and cloud, and a rainbow finale. The backcloth was hung with strip lights to represent both rain and Mandy's felt-tip pens, and each one was a different colour of the rainbow. In different scenes, different and appropriate lights were lit, and only for the finale did all the lights illuminate to create a rainbow effect.

The backcloth was also lit with projections. Upstage was a large cloud shape covered with white silk, which had steps behind it, and a rainbow lightbox inside. This also received images from the projectors; in the swimming pool scene, a backstage fan made the cloud's silk ripple like water. There was a grey dancefloor on the stage, with raindrops painted on it.

Stage Furniture

ACT ONE

- A bed with Mandy's duvet, a beanbag, and a chair.
- A table and three chairs.
- Two small overhead projectors (epidiascopes) at the front of the stage on either side, to draw on and from which images are projected onto the flat surfaces on the stage.

ACT TWO

- The bed was covered with an indigo-coloured bedspread. The rest of the stage was clear.
- Three mannequins were added to the Indigo shop scene.

Costume rails were also used in the original production, which were wheeled in and out:

- A long rail for Mandy's bedroom, hung with pocket holders full of toy monkeys. The reverse side was used for the green dream scene, and later, decorated with library pictures for the library.
- A long rail of dresses for the Mandy and Mum shopping scene, and later, for Tanya's bedroom, hung with indigo holders containing stolen items.
- A short rail with a hospital screen on one side and curtains on the other to represent Mandy's window.
- Three short rails dressed with assorted accessories at the start of the shopping centre scene.

Costume Design

The costumes in the original production were all designed for quick changes, since many of the actors were playing multiple characters. The dresses in the dream sequences were designed like cut-out doll's dresses with tabs. They hung like aprons, with velcro fastenings and could be put on and taken off easily.

Music

In the original production, we used excerpts from current popular music, familiar to the age-range of the audience and relevant to the particular scene it was used in.

This play is dedicated with my love and admiration to Jacqueline Wilson, Nick Sharratt and everyone involved in the original production, plus huge thanks to Polka Theatre and Watershed Productions.

VICKY IRELAND

Bad Girls was commissioned by and first performed at Polka Theatre, Wimbledon, London, on 24 June 2004, then toured by Watershed Productions throughout the UK. The cast was as follows:

MANDY	Susan Harrison
KIM	Alison Thea-Skot
ARTHUR	Francois Pandolfo
TANYA	Luanna Priestman
MUM (MORAG)	Sally Armstrong
DAD (TOM)	Peter Sowerbutts
ASST STAGE MANAGERS / UNDERSTUDIES	Zoë Bond
	Rebecca Shorrocks
	Ben Tyreman

Director   Vicky Ireland
Designer   Bridget Kimak
Lighting Designer   Ian Scott
Composer and Sound Designer   Steven Markwick
Choreographer   Ben Redfern

FOR POLKA THEATRE, WIMBLEDON, LONDON
Artistic Director   Annie Wood
Administrative Director   Stephen Midlane

FOR WATERSHED PRODUCTIONS
Executive Producer   Chris Wallis
Producer and General Manager   Elizabeth Jones

BAD GIRLS

Characters (*in order of appearance*)

KIM MATTHEWS
MELANIE HOLDER
SARAH NEWMAN
ARTHUR KING
MANDY WHITE
MORAG WHITE (MUM)
TOM WHITE (DAD)
TANYA
MRS STANLEY
MRS EDWARDS
SERGEANT STOCKTON
MR MOSELEY

WOMAN
BUS DRIVER
PARAMEDIC
NURSE
CLAPPERBOARD
INTERVIEWER
JOURNALIST
CLASS MONITOR
ICE-CREAM VENDOR
ANNOUNCER
SHOP ASSISTANT
SECURITY GUARD
POLICEMAN
POLICEWOMAN
LIBRARIAN
CHILDREN (ZAP *and* POW)
TV CREW
SCHOOLCHILDREN
MODELS
SHOPPERS

ACT ONE

Scene One
RED

Bus stop. Morning.

Music. A roll of thunder. KIM *enters, followed by* MELANIE *and* SARAH. *They stand at a bus stop.* ARTHUR *enters and reads a book.* MANDY *enters, looking scared.* KIM *bumps into* MANDY.

KIM. She's trying to ignore us! Did Mumsie-Wumsie tell you to ignore us rude nasty girlies, then? Where is Mumsie, anyway? Hey, I'm talking to you! Mandy White. You deaf or something? WHERE'S MUMSIE?

ARTHUR *stops reading and watches the girls.*

MANDY. She's at the dentist's.

KIM. Oooh, at the *dentist's*. Well, she needs to go there. She's so wrinkly and grey and ancient I reckon her teeth are all rotten and skanky and she needs false ones.

MANDY. You shut up about my mum.

KIM. How old was she when she had you, Mandy? Sixty, seventy, a hundred?

MANDY. You're just being stupid. My mum's not that old.

KIM. So how old is she, then?

MANDY. None of your business.

MELANIE. She's fifty-five. And her dad's even older, he's sixty-two.

SARAH. That's ancient!

They mime old people hobbling about.

MANDY. Stop it!

KIM. Oooh look, she's gone all red. So what's Daddy like, then? Is he all googly-eyed and ga-ga?

MELANIE. He's got this silly beard and he wears a smock.

KIM. A *smock*! Like a frock? Mandy's dad wears a *frock!*

MANDY. A smock *isn't* a frock. Fishermen wear them. Daddy just wears it when he's painting.

MELANIE/SARAH/KIM. 'Daddy'!

MANDY. Yes, well, all right, I have to call them Daddy and Mummy because they make me. But they're not my real mum and dad.

KIM (*hands on hips*). What are you on about?

MANDY. And my real name's not Mandy White. I was adopted as a baby. I've met my real mum, and she's amazing: she's a fashion model, you'd know her name but I'm not allowed to say it. Anyway, she was very young and it was going to interfere with her career, so she had me adopted but she's always kept in touch and she sends me wonderful presents, all sorts of clothes and shoes and stuff, but my adopted mum doesn't approve and locks them away in trunks and makes me wear all this baby stuff . . .

MELANIE. You liar! That's not true, I've been round to your house and there aren't any trunks –

MANDY. No, they're in the loft. I swear.

MELANIE. Well, you shouldn't because I *know* it's a lie. Your mum told my mum how she tried for ages to have a baby and they tried to adopt but they were too old, then she suddenly started you. 'Our little miracle baby.' That's what she said. So you're a *liar*!

KIM. Liar!

MANDY *tries to move.*

Oh no, you're not going anywhere Mandy Miracle-Babe Loony-Liar.

MELANIE. Liar.

SARAH. Liar, liar, pants-on-fire.

KIM. Yeah, what colour pants have you got on today, Mandy?

KIM *pulls up* MANDY*'s skirt.*

MANDY. Stop it, stop it. (MANDY *clutches her skirt.*)

KIM. Oh, how *sweet*. White with little rabbits on! To match the itsy-bitsy bunnies Mumsie knitted on your cardie. Poor Mumsie, knitting and knitting for naughty Miracle-Mandy – when she goes round telling everyone she's adopted! Mumsie's going to be soooo-oo upset when she finds out.

MANDY. How will she find out?

KIM. Well, I'll ask her tomorrow, when she comes to collect you. 'How old was Mandy when you adopted her, Mrs White?' and she'll say, 'Oh, Mandy's my own little girl, dear' and I'll say, 'That's not what Mandy says. *She* swears she's adopted.'

MANDY. You're wicked, wicked, wicked!

MANDY *slaps* KIM's *face hard. Music.*

KIM. Get her.

KIM, MELANIE *and* SARAH *chase* MANDY *offstag*e.

The road.

A bus starts to approach. MANDY *re-enters.* ARTHUR *waves his arms to warn* MANDY.

ARTHUR. Mandy, Mandy . . . stop!

There is the screech of brakes. MANDY *falls. Her glasses are knocked off.*

Scene Two
ORANGE

MANDY *is lying on the ground.* ARTHUR *is kneeling by her. A* WOMAN *and a* BUS DRIVER *enter.*

WOMAN. Oh my goodness!

They attend to MANDY, *who sits up and clutches her broken glasses.*

BUS DRIVER. She just ran into the road, I only just stopped in time.

A PARAMEDIC *enters.*

PARAMEDIC. Stand back everybody, please, I need to come through. She'll be fine.

WOMAN and BUS DRIVER exit.

Hello young lady, what's your name?

MANDY. Mandy.

PARAMEDIC. I'm going to sit you down and I want you to keep that arm very still for me, OK?

She helps MANDY to sit as a NURSE enters with a sling.

Hospital.

NURSE. Mandy White? Now there's no broken bones, it's just a bad sprain. You'll need to rest your arm for a day or so.

She puts the sling on MANDY's arm.

Your mum's on her way.

MUM enters.

MUM. Mandy! Oh my lamb.

NURSE exits. MANDY and MUM move to MANDY's bedroom.

MANDY's bedroom. MANDY changes into pyjamas behind screen.

DAD enters.

Oh Tom, it was awful at the hospital, I was so frightened.

DAD. Well, I got away from work as fast as I could.

MANDY is now in bed with her arm in a sling. MUM gives her an orange drink. MANDY hands over her glasses to DAD.

MANDY. I'm ever so sorry I broke my glasses.

DAD. Just so long as you're safe and sound, poppet. What a pair. Poor Mum, poor Mandy. (*To* MUM.) All that horrid stuff at the dentist, (*To* MANDY.) and then you bump into a bus.

MUM. She didn't just 'bump into a bus', she was chased by some girls.

DAD. Which girls?

MUM. It's those three again, isn't it? Melanie and that really nasty big girl and the short one. I can't understand how Melanie can be so horrid, she seemed such a nice girl, and I really got on well with her mother. I'm going to phone her –

MANDY. No!

MUM. We'll have to go to the school and tell your teacher –

MANDY. *No!* You can't!

DAD. Now, now, calm down, sweetheart. Hey, you're spilling your orange. (*He takes the orange drink.*) Why are you getting in such a state? Are you really scared of these girls?

MUM. Of *course* she's scared, poor little thing. So scared she ran into the road. Oh dear, when I *think* what could have happened! She could have gone under the bus and –

DAD. Mandy, you've got to tell us exactly what these girls did.

MANDY. They didn't do anything! I wish you'd stop going on about it. And you mustn't tell their mums or anyone at school or else –

DAD. Or else what, pet?

MANDY. They'll all hate me.

   DAD *uses toy monkey Olivia to wipe her tears, then* MANDY *takes it.*

MUM. Don't be silly, how could anyone hate you? You're a lovely girl. They're just jealous because you always come top. I know Melanie's mother was worried her divorce had unsettled Melanie. But still, that's no excuse for bullying, chasing you right out into the road.

MANDY. It *wasn't* Melanie, it was Kim –

DAD. Which one's that?

MUM. The tall girl – the one who looks much older than her age. I've always thought she was a nasty piece of work. I've heard her say some silly things behind *my* back. So what was she saying this afternoon?

MANDY. I can't remember.

MUM. Come along, Mandy, we've never had secrets in our family.

DAD. You can tell us anything.

MANDY. I really truly can't remember. It's making my head hurt just thinking about it. Can't I go to sleep? Please?

Music. The parents exit. MANDY *falls asleep and dreams she is* MIRANDA RAINBOW. *A* TV CREW *enters. This sequence should be updated to refer to current pop groups.*

CLAPPERBOARD. Standing by, please. Going in 5, 4, 3 – *(Mouths silently.)* 2, 1 – *(Snaps clapperboard.)*

INTERVIEWER *(to camera)*. Hi there! Today's interview is with that talented and glamorous superstar, the wonderful Miss Miranda Rainbow. So Miranda, tell us something about the house.

MANDY. My house was designed by top New York designers and it has fifteen bathrooms and each one has a solid gold bath in it. I live here with my parents, Nick and Kate, and both of them are twenty-nine years old. And my dad Nick manages a boy band and the band comes over all the time because they all fancy me.

INTERVIEWER. Fabulous!

CLAPPERBOARD. Cut! OK, make-up, hair! She looks fabulous, make her look better. Standing by. Going in 5, 4, 3 – (2, 1 –) *(Snaps clapperboard.)*

INTERVIEWER. So tell us about your new album, *All the Colours of Miranda.*

MANDY. I completed my album last month at Kylie Minogue's studio and we hung out together and ate pizza and I tried on all her shoes. And my album is really a collaboration between myself and Busted and now all three members of Busted are my boyfriends.

INTERVIEWER. Even the one with the eyebrows?

MANDY. Especially him!

INTERVIEWER. Fabulous.

CLAPPERBOARD. Right, get her sorted then we'll take questions from the floor. Going in 5, 4, 3 – (2, 1 –) *(Snaps clapperboard.)*

INTERVIEWER. We have some questions from the floor.

JOURNALIST. Yes – Miranda. I have a photograph of you in the playground and you're on your own. You don't have any friends.

MANDY. No, that's not me.

INTERVIEWER. And I'm getting a report through that your name isn't Miranda Rainbow, it's Mandy White and you wear glasses!

MANDY. No, that's not me.

The CREW *exit muttering 'four eyes'.* MANDY *gets back into bed and tosses around.*

I'm Miranda Rainbow, I'm not Mandy White.

Morning. MUM *enters.*

MUM. Morning, sweetheart. Bad dreams?

MANDY. Yes.

MUM (*hands* MANDY *her glasses*). Daddy's superglued your glasses. Oh, you still look peaky. I think you'd better have a quiet day in bed, just to be on the safe side. I think I'll take the day too. Say I'm sick. It's not really a fib. My teeth are still playing up.

MANDY. But you can go to work, Mummy. I'll be fine on my own.

MUM. I'd much rather stay at home with you, darling. I'll go and ring them now and I'll make us a nice cup of tea.

MUM *exits.* MANDY *picks up Gertrude, her toy gorilla, and talks to her.*

MANDY. Why does Mummy have to stay at home too, it's so boring.

Music. TANYA *enters with a baby in a buggy.* MANDY *looks through her window and sees her.* TANYA *stops and catches sight of* MANDY *and waves.* MANDY *is startled.* TANYA *exits. Music fades.*

Scene Three
YELLOW

Home.

MANDY *moves to living room.* MUM *enters with two mugs of tea. The phone rings.*

MUM. Mrs White speaking. Oh. Yes, hold on. Mandy, it's for you. It's a boy!

MUM *hands phone to* MANDY.

MANDY. Hello?

ARTHUR *enters holding a phone. He is also clutching a book on King Arthur with a yellow cover.*

ARTHUR. Hi Mandy, it's Arthur, Arthur King. Sorry I haven't rung before. So they didn't keep you in hospital long. Have you broken anything? Remember when I broke my leg last year and I had that plaster cast and everyone wrote stuff all over it, even poems, remember that rude one?

MANDY. I've hurt my wrist, but it's not broken, so I've just got a sling. You can't write on it 'cos it's material.

ARTHUR. Oh well. Never mind. I mean, I'm ever so glad you're all right.

MANDY. Mmmm.

ARTHUR. You're *sure* you're all right? You haven't got concussion, have you? You're not saying very much.

MANDY. You're not giving me a chance.

ARTHUR *(laughs)*. Mandy?

MANDY. Yes?

ARTHUR. Mmm. Mandy?

MANDY. What?

ARTHUR. I feel bad about yesterday. I just stood there. While they were saying all that stuff.

MANDY. Well, they weren't saying it about you.

ARTHUR. Yes, but I should have rescued you.

MANDY. You what?

ARTHUR. It wasn't very chivalrous.

MANDY. You what?

MUM. Will you stop using that horrible uncouth expression. Who *is* this boy?

MANDY (*to* MUM). Arthur's in my class at school.

ARTHUR. I know I'm in your class at school. I think you *have* got concussion.

MANDY. No, I was just telling my mum who you are, that's all.

MUM. Your tea's getting cold. Come along, say bye bye.

MANDY. I've got to go in a minute. Shiver-what?

ARTHUR. What?

MANDY. You said you weren't shivering or something. Yesterday.

ARTHUR. No – chivalrous! Like a knight. Like my namesake King Arthur. I didn't rescue the damsel in distress, did I? I just stood there and I *was* shivering. Scared. Cowardly custard. (*Looks down at the cover of his book.*) Yellow. That was me.

MANDY. It's OK, Arthur. Really. Anyway, I'm a coward too.

ARTHUR. Yes, but it's all right for you, you're a girl.

MANDY. Look, we're not back in those days. Girls aren't supposed to be rescued now. We're meant to sort ourselves out.

ARTHUR. But there were three of them and only one of you. I'm a rotten coward. And I'm sorry. I'm ever so sorry.

MANDY. That's quite all right. I have to get on with my tea now. Bye.

ARTHUR. Bye.

ARTHUR *exits.* MANDY *puts the phone down and drinks her tea.*

MUM. So what shall we do with the rest of the day? I really should be at work. Oh Mandy, aren't we bad girls! We could do some baking together. It would be a nice surprise for Daddy when he comes home from work. How about some fairy cakes, you like them, with icing on the top?

MANDY. Oh yeah, can we have some of those hundreds and thousands on top?

MUM. Yes, if there's some in the cupboard left over from Christmas, and then we could make some gingerbread men?

MANDY. Yeah! Great idea.

Music. MUM *and* MANDY *cook. Music fades.*

MUM. I'll bring you a bun when they're cool. You go and have a rest.

MANDY. But I don't want a rest.

MUM *exits.*

Boring!

Music. MANDY *sits on her bed and looks out of the window.* TANYA *enters with shopping bags. She is wearing a Kurt Cobain T-shirt. She sees* MANDY.

TANYA. Open the window!

MANDY. Can't. Childproof locks.

TANYA *shrugs, waves and exits.* MANDY *sits in a dream.* MUM *enters with a plate of fairy cakes.*

MUM. Mandy, stop mooning about. Try a fairy cake, eh? Come on, sweetheart, cheer up.

MANDY. Mummy, can I have my hair cut?

MUM. Oh darling, don't be silly. Your hair's lovely.

MANDY. No, it's not. And I don't want plaits any more, *no one* has plaits these days. Can't I have my hair short – and sort of sticking up?

MUM. Like a bird's nest!

MANDY. Mummy, has Mrs Williams over the road got any daughters? Real ones, I mean, not the foster babies. (*She licks her cake.*)

MUM. Don't eat it like that, pet. Yes, I think she's got one grown-up daughter in Canada.

MANDY. This girl isn't grown up.

MUM. Which girl?

MANDY. The girl I saw earlier on and just now. She was helping with one of the babies and doing the shopping.

MUM. Maybe she's got a granddaughter. About your age?

MANDY. No, older.

MUM. Still, it would be nice if you had someone to make friends with, now that Melanie's turned so silly. Tell you what, how about taking some of the cakes over?

MANDY. No, Mummy! I don't want to.

MUM. Don't be so soppy.

She hands MANDY *the plate of cakes.*

Here! Over you go.

MANDY. No, Mum. Please. I feel stupid.

MUM. You are a funny little poppet. Shall I come with you?

MANDY. I don't want to go at all.

MUM. Oh all right, then I'll pop over. (MUM *exits.*)

MANDY (*picks up* GERTRUDE). Oh Gertrude, why am I so useless? Not surprised they call me names. I bet Kim's making up some more stupid ones right now. I never want to go to school ever again. I feel sick. (*She crams cake in her mouth.*)

MUM *enters, shocked.*

MUM. Oh dear, oh dear, that was a bit awkward. You didn't tell me what this Tanya was *like.*

MANDY. Tanya!

MUM. Do you know, she actually calls Mrs Williams 'Pat' – not even *Auntie* Pat. Though of course she's not related. She's a foster child. But whatever does she *look* like!

MANDY. I think she looks really cool.

MUM. She wanted to ask you over to play, but I said you weren't well and you were having a lie-down.

MANDY. *Mum!*

MUM. Well, you were the one that didn't want to go over.

MANDY. Yes, but – if she *wants* me to . . .

MUM. Well, I'd much rather you didn't. A girl like that! You haven't got anything in common. And she's much older than you. The clothes she's wearing! I hope Mrs Williams knows what she's taking on.

TANYA (*offstage*). Coo-ee?

TANYA enters with the plate, empty.

Hiya! It's only me, Tanya. Door was open. Thanks for the little cakes, they were smashing.

MUM. You haven't eaten them all?

TANYA. You bet I have. Well, the others just licked the icing off theirs, so I got lucky. You're Mandy, right? Let's have a chat, then.

MUM. Well, I really think Mandy ought to have a rest just now. Perhaps another time.

TANYA laughs.

TANYA. But she's *had* a rest, haven't you, Mandy? You want me to play, don't you? Show us your bedroom, then.

MUM. Well, just for ten minutes. She's got school tomorrow.

Music. MUM exits. The girls move to MANDY's bedroom. Music fades.

TANYA. Wow! It's all pink and pretty and girlie. How do you keep it so clean? Oh, and I like your *bed*! (*She leaps on it.*) Mmm, it smells clean too. Hello? (*She picks up Olivia.*) Who's this, then?

MANDY. That's one of my monkeys. I have this monkey collection.

TANYA. Let's see.

MANDY shows her collection of toy monkeys to TANYA, who plays with them.

They're great.

MANDY. And there's this one –

She indicates Gertrude. TANYA picks her up.

TANYA. I like him. He tickles. (*Puts her down and picks up Olivia.*) This one's still my favourite.

MANDY. She's mine too. Her name's Olivia.

TANYA. Hello Olivia. Haven't you got a posh name? Ooooh yes, I should jolly well say so. (*Puts Olivia on her head.*) She's got the same hair colour as me! Do you like it?

MANDY. I think it's brilliant.

TANYA. It's not *really* this colour. Just sort of mouse. 'Cept that's boring.

MANDY. Yes.

TANYA. I thought I might go black some time. All Gothic and witchy. What do you think? Or blonde like you. You've got lovely hair.

MANDY. Me?

TANYA. My little sister Carmel's got long hair too. Just like yours. You look like her. I thought you were her for a minute when I saw you up at the window. Mad, eh? I used to do our Carmel's hair every day. I'm good at long hair. I'll do yours for you, if you like.

MANDY. *Would* you?

TANYA. Sure.

MANDY. There is a brush and clip under the bed. (*She gets them out, plus a small hand mirror.*)

TANYA. Excellent. Make yourself comfortable.

Music. MANDY *sits.* TANYA *brushes her hair.*

I'm ever so gentle, 'cos Carmel yells her head off if you tug her tangles. You're *much* better behaved.

MANDY. Is Carmel at Mrs Williams too?

Music fades. Pause.

TANYA. You can get all sorts of slides and bands if you want to wear it up. Carmel used to have heaps. I did my little brothers' hair too, kept them looking really nice. I've got two brothers, Sean and Matty. And my Carmel. I looked after them like I was their mum. There.

TANYA *passes* MANDY *the mirror.*

Like it?

MANDY. Oh wow!

TANYA. That's why they're trying me out at Pat's 'cos I'm good with little kids. I hoped she'd have girls but there's Simon and that gormless Charlie and baby Ricky and they *all* yell and muck around and play with their willies.

MANDY *laughs.*

I'm sick of little boys *and* big boys. Me and my boyfriend broke up three weeks ago, and do you know something, it's the best thing that's ever happened to me, because he is a pig. Yeah, all boys give me the creeps. So that's why I thought I'd make friends with a little girl instead.

MANDY. I'm not actually a *little* girl.

TANYA. You're tiny! Still, I'm small too. Without my heels.

She sees MANDY *looking at her shoes.*

You can try them on if you want.

MANDY. *Can* I?

She puts TANYA*'s shoes on.*

They're a bit big, I've never worn heels before.

TANYA. OK, pout your lips, stick out your bum and we're off. Strut!

MANDY *struts as* MUM *enters with a tray of Ribena and gingerbread men.*

MUM. Mandy! Watch your ankles. It's not very nice to try on other people's shoes. What ever have you done to your hair?

MANDY. Tanya did it. I think it looks fantastic.

MUM. Hm. I thought you might like a drink and a snack. Before you go home. (*She puts the tray down.*) Though I expect you're still full up with cake.

TANYA. Ooh no, I'm always starving – even though I stay so skinny. Is this Coke?

MUM. No, it's Ribena actually. And some gingerbread men. Home-made.

TANYA. Gingerbread *folk*. We made them at this home I was in, and it's sexist to call them men, because women wear trousers too, don't they? (*She nibbles off the legs.*) There, she's wearing shorts now!

MANDY (*does the same*). I've got a woman too.

MUM. Mandy, don't talk with your mouth full.

MANDY. You can go now, Mum.

   MUM *exits.*

TANYA. You hungry?

   TANYA *feeds Gertrude, then feeds the man on her T-shirt.*

   Here, Kurt, you have a mouthful.

MANDY. Who?

TANYA. You don't know who Kurt Cobain is? Only the greatest rock star ever, and I just love him.

MANDY. I thought you hated boys.

TANYA. He's not a boy, Miss Clever-Clogs.

MANDY. Well, a man then.

TANYA. He's not a man either. He's an angel, because he's dead. Or a devil.

MANDY. He's dead?

TANYA. He committed suicide. What else do you have under here. (*She looks under the bed and pulls out a large pack of felt-tip pens.*) Wow! Do these felt-tips work?

MANDY. Yes.

TANYA. Let's draw, then. I *love* colouring. (*She starts to draw her mother as an angel.*) This is me mum –

MANDY. Where is your mum, Tanya, why don't you live with her?

TANYA. She committed suicide. She topped herself.

MANDY. How . . . awful.

   Music.

TANYA. Well, she was always a bit zonked out of her brains.

It's OK, it was ages ago, but I can still remember her. She's an angel now and that's why she's got wings.

She finishes her drawing. Music fades.

There.

MANDY. That's brilliant.

TANYA. Your turn.

MANDY. I don't know what to draw. I'm not drawing my mum.

TANYA. Draw me, then.

MANDY. OK. I'll do your face first and your T-shirt. Here are your eyes and you've got a big smile and the coolest thing about you, 1, 2, 3 – your hair! (*She finishes her drawing.*)

TANYA. I look wicked. OK, I'll draw you now. I'll start with your long golden hair, then your face and your glasses –

MANDY. Err!

TANYA. And I'll make it a sunny day.

She draws a sun around MANDY*'s head.*

MANDY. Yeah.

TANYA (*writing around the sun*). 'My Frend Mandy.' Do you like it?

MANDY. I love it.

Music. TANYA *sits on the bed then starts to bounce on it.*

TANYA. Come on, let's bounce!

MANDY *is not too sure, then joins in. They both whoop with joy.*

They exit.

Scene Four
GREEN

The playground.

The morning school bell rings. ARTHUR *enters.*

ARTHUR (*calls off*). Ta-ra Mam.

He stumbles and drops his books, then talks to himself as he picks them up.

Now, I have to get my story right. I'm King Arthur with my shining armour and my special sword and I'm going to slay the evil dragon of Llandoff, because, because – inside his heart is a . . .

MANDY *and* MUM *enter and stand next to him.*

Hi Mandy's mum. (*He exits.*)

MANDY. Bye Mummy. I can go into school on my own. You don't have to stay.

MUM. No, I've brought you to school for a reason. I'm going to make sure things are sorted out.

MUM *marches across the playground.* MANDY *dashes after.*

MANDY. Mummy, please, promise you won't say anything to Mrs Stanley.

MUM. I'm not talking to your form teacher, I'm going to have a little word with the head.

MANDY. The head! Mum, you *can't* tell Mrs Edwards. They'll all hate me and think I'm a sneaky telltale.

MUM. Don't be silly, darling. I just need to let Mrs Edwards know what's happening in her school.

MUM *exits.*

MANDY. But you can't, you don't understand . . .

Classroom.

KIM *enters and threatens* MANDY. MELANIE *and* SARAH *enter and watch.*

KIM. Right, Mandy White, I want a word with you – Just seen your beloved mother wiggling into school. So what's she want, eh? Come on, babywaby – tell us or you're going to be in trouble, you little four eyes, snobby swot –

MRS STANLEY *enters.*

MRS STANLEY. Quiet, please. (*They all sit.*) Good morning, class.

CLASS. Good morning, Mrs Stanley.

MRS STANLEY. Right, settle down everyone, ready for registration, please.

CLASS MONITOR *enters.*

MONITOR. Excuse me, Mrs Stanley, but Mrs Edwards wants to see Kim Matthews, Melanie Holder and Sarah Newman straight away. She wants them to wait in the corridor outside her office.

MANDY *cowers.*

MRS STANLEY. Oh dear.

KIM *stands and hovers behind* MANDY*'s chair.*

Off you go then, you three. I hope you haven't been up to something stupid.

KIM, MELANIE *and* SARAH *exit.*

What's the matter, Mandy? Why are you sitting like that, dear? Have you got a tummy ache? Do you need to go to the toilet?

MANDY *nods.*

Well, why didn't you say so, you silly girl? Really, you're not a baby, Mandy. Off you go, then.

MANDY *exits the classroom in tears and enters the girls' toilets.* CLASS MONITOR *enters.*

MONITOR. Mandy White, are you in there? You've got to come out 'cos you've been in there ages and Mrs Stanley says if you're really not well you'd better go to the office, and you've got to go to the office *anyway* because Mrs Edwards wants you.

MANDY. Just coming.

MANDY *comes out of the toilets.*

MONITOR. What were you *doing* in there? Were you being sick?

MANDY. No.

MONITOR. Well, you look sick. Come *on*, then.

Music. The CLASS MONITOR *and* MANDY *make their way to the headteacher's office. They pass* KIM, SARAH *and* MELANIE *who are waiting outside and enter as* MRS EDWARDS *enters.*

MRS EDWARDS. Thank you, Duncan!

MONITOR *exits*.

Come in, Mandy, sit down. (*She does so.*) I hear you've been having an unhappy time at school recently? You've certainly done very well at your lessons, and you've seemed happy and cheerful enough. But for a while now there have been some girls who have been upsetting you?

MANDY *bends lower*.

Mandy! Sit up straight, please. It's Kim and Sarah and Melanie, isn't it? Your mother says they've been tormenting you. And last Wednesday they chased you into the road and you were knocked down by a bus? Is this true? Because if it is, it needs to be dealt with. Did they chase you?

MANDY. Sort of.

MRS EDWARDS *looks into the corridor and indicates the three girls to enter.*

MRS EDWARDS. In here, you three!

They enter.

Mandy here is being incredibly loyal to you girls, but it is obvious to me that you've been very unkind and this has got to stop, do you hear? I detest bullying. I won't have it in my school. Now Kim, Melanie, Sarah, I want you to say you're sorry and promise that you won't bully Mandy ever again.

MELANIE *starts to speak but* KIM *interrupts her.*

KIM. I think Mandy should say sorry to us. It was just as much her fault telling stories about her mum being a fashion model –

MRS EDWARDS. Don't be ridiculous, Kim. Don't make things worse for yourself by telling silly lies.

KIM. I'm not lying, Mrs Edwards. You *did* say that, didn't you, Mandy?

MANDY *bends her head.*

MRS EDWARDS. Mandy?

SARAH. It was Mandy who told the lies, Mrs Edwards.

KIM. And when we told her we knew she was lying, she got really mad and she shouted at us and then she hit me.

MRS EDWARDS. Now, really, Kim, you can't expect me to believe that. Mandy's half your size.

KIM. She still hit me. Really hard.

SARAH. She did, Mrs Edwards. She punched Kim straight in the face.

KIM. And then she ran away and wasn't looking where she was going and got hit by the bus. It was all *Mandy*, Mrs Edwards.

MRS EDWARDS. You didn't hit Kim, did you? Just tell the truth, dear.

MANDY. Yes, I did.

The school bell rings.

MRS EDWARDS. Oh, the bell, well . . . I still find it very difficult to believe this. However, I know that you three have been ganging up on Mandy recently. It's got to stop. You're not to call her names or say anything horrid to her, do you understand?

KIM. Oh yes, Mrs Edwards, we understand. We won't say *anything* to Mandy.

MRS EDWARDS. Good. (*She exits.*)

KIM *smiles slyly. Music.* ARTHUR *enters with his King Arthur book and watches. The girls form frozen pictures to show they are not talking to* MANDY. *Music fades.* MELANIE *and* SARAH *exit.* KIM *hovers.* ARTHUR *moves over to* MANDY.

ARTHUR. Hi Mandy, are you all right?

MANDY (*upset*). Yes.

KIM *sniggers.*

ARTHUR (*to* KIM). Leave us alone. (*To* MANDY.) Come on, let's go over here. You know I was telling you about my namesake, King Arthur. Well, I've been thinking about writing my own story about him. (*He shows her his book.*) That's King Arthur there and this is the princess. (*Looks at her.*) Would you like to be the princess?

MANDY. OK, just for a minute before my mum comes.

ARTHUR. Yes!

Music. KIM *watches in the background.*

So I'm King Arthur, with my shining armour, just pretend,
and I get on my black horse and ride through the night,
through bushes and briars in the forest. Then I get off my
horse, gracefully, and hand the horse to the princess, that's
you, and I get out my special sword and I slay the dragon.
He breathes fire, see, so you got to be careful. Then I kill
him, take out his heart and inside his heart is a stone and I
give that to the princess –

He kneels in front of MANDY.

– and bow in honour of the round table, 'cos I saved the
soul of the princess.

KIM *moves forward and laughs in his face.*

KIM. Derrrr!

ARTHUR *exits in embarrassment.* KIM *starts to approach*
MANDY *as* MUM *enters.*

MUM. Mandy, hello poppet. So, what did Mrs Edwards say?

MANDY. *Sssh,* Mum.

MUM. Did she give that Kim a good telling off?

MANDY. Please, Mummy. Don't let's talk about it now.

MUM. That's her, isn't it? Well, she doesn't look very sorry.
Maybe I'd better have a few words with that young madam.

MANDY. No, Mummy, please. Mrs Edwards sorted it all out
and they've promised they won't say anything else.

MUM. Are you *sure*? You still look very bothered, darling.

MANDY. I'm not bothered at all. Let's go home.

Music. MANDY *and* MUM *leave school.* ARTHUR *and*
KIM *follow.* MUM *exits.* TANYA *enters with a baby buggy.*

Tanya!

Music fades.

TANYA. Hey, Mandy! How was school?

MANDY *pulls a face.*

I get you. I can't stick school. Still, I don't have to go as it's the school holidays soon. All them stupid teachers. And silly kids calling you names.

MANDY. They call *you* names?

TANYA. Yeah, but I call them worse. Why, anyone giving you hassle?

KIM *approaches*.

What are you staring at?

KIM. Nothing.

TANYA. Well, run off home, little girlie. Leave me and my pal Mandy in peace.

KIM *and* ARTHUR *exit*.

I'm taking His Lordship for a walk around the park. Coming?

MUM *enters, puffing*.

MANDY. Mum, can I go to the park with Tanya, please?

MUM. I don't think so. You can get funny men hanging around there. It's no place for young girls on their own.

TANYA. I'll look after Mandy, don't worry.

MUM. No dear, another time perhaps.

MANDY. But I want to go *today*, Mummy. It's not fair. Why do you have to treat me like a baby all the time? Mrs Edwards said I should be more independent. She thinks I'm too young for my age and that's why the others pick on me.

MUM. Don't be silly.

TANYA. We'll be back in half an hour.

MUM. Oh, all right. If you really want to go to the park, we'll walk along with Tanya.

MANDY. No. You don't have to come with us, Mum. There's no main roads or anything. And we'll keep away from funny men. All the others go to the park by themselves.

MUM. All right, but just for half an hour.

Music. MUM *exits.* MANDY *and* TANYA *'high five' then walk to the park. Music fades into the sound of birdsong.*

TANYA. Mmm, it's lovely here. So green and quiet. Oh dear, Baby's been a bit sicky. (*She wipes the baby's face.*) That's it, Ricky. Sticky, sticky, Ricky.

MANDY. My daddy used to bring me here when I was little. We went on the swings and paddled in the paddling pool. It was really good fun.

TANYA. Your dad sounds nice. (*To baby.*) Now keep still, little one.

MANDY. Mmm. But my mum's a bit . . . (*She pulls a face.*)

TANYA. She fusses because she cares about you. I used to fuss about Carmel heaps.

MANDY. Do you miss her a lot?

TANYA. Yeah. Still, I've got you instead now, haven't I, young Mandy?

MANDY. I'm not *young* Mandy.

TANYA (*laughs and pulls her plaits*). You look about six with these.

MANDY. Don't. I asked my mum to do it the way you did, but she wouldn't.

TANYA. Then learn to do it yourself. I'd better put Ricky in the shade.

She puts the buggy to the side. A VENDOR *enters with a cart.*

There. But we can do a spot of sunbathing, eh? (*She lies down on the grass.*) I've got to get my tummy brown.

MANDY. I don't go brown, just pink. I hate pink. It's my worst colour in all the world.

TANYA. Well, we'll just lie in the sun for two minutes. Don't want you burning.

Music. MANDY *lies down too, head to head with* TANYA.

MANDY. I'm so happy you're my friend. I used to be friends with Melanie, but then she went off with Kim and left me on my own. It was awful.

TANYA. Well, you're not on your own any more.

Music fades.

Hey, you look really hot. I'll get some ice cream.

She crosses to the VENDOR.

Hiya, two cones, please.

As the VENDOR *bends to the make the ice creams,* TANYA *notices some hair scrunchies amongst other things attached to the side of the stall. She looks around, then puts her hand out slowly to steal one. As the* VENDOR *straightens and hands her two cones, she straightens too.*

VENDOR. That'll be one pound fifty, please.

TANYA hands him a note. As he bends to get the change, she steals the top green scrunchie. MANDY *has seen the theft and is shocked.*

There's your change. (*He hands her the change.*)

TANYA. Thanks. Bye.

TANYA crosses back to MANDY *and hands her an ice cream, then looks at* MANDY'*s watch.*

Look at the time. Come on, we'd better get you home. Can't have your mum fussing.

Music. The VENDOR *exits. The girls journey home. Music fades.*

Here we are home, safe and sound. Oh – got you a little present.

TANYA takes out the scrunchie.

It's called a scrunchie, for your hair. Like this. Take your plaits out.

MANDY. Oh, I'm not sure. Do you think it'll really suit me?

TANYA (*puts MANDY's hair into the scrunchie*). Yeah, everyone'll want their hair like this when they see you. It's so cool. There! Green really suits you. Looks wicked.

MANDY. Does it? Yeah, it's wicked. Thanks, Tanya. I love my scrunchie.

TANYA. Good. See you later.

MANDY. Yeah, see ya.

TANYA exits.

Scene Five
BLUE

Home.

MUM *and* DAD *enter.* MANDY *approaches them.*

MANDY. Look, Mummy, what do you think? (*She shows them her hair.*) Tanya did it and she bought me the scrunchie.

MUM. I know you think you look wonderful. But I don't think that style really suits you.

DAD. I think she looks very grown up.

MUM. That's just the point. Mandy's still a little girl. That style's much too sophisticated. And a bit common, if you ask me.

DAD. Still, it was kind of Tanya to give her the hair thingy.

MUM. Mmm. Did she buy it for you specially?

MANDY. Yes. (*She pretends to yawn.*) Oh, I'm ever so sleepy. I think I'll go to bed.

MUM. But you haven't had your tea?

MANDY. Don't worry, I had an ice cream. I don't want anything else.

DAD. It's all that sun, I expect. Night night, poppet.

MANDY. Night Dad. (*Kisses him.*) Mum.

She goes to her bedroom.

MUM. It's not like her to miss her tea, I'll just settle her down.

MUM *goes to the bedroom.*

DAD. Oh Morag! (*He sighs and exits.*)

MUM. Mandy . . . (*She turns down the bed.*) I've just come to settle you down, sweetheart.

MANDY *appears in her pyjamas and gets into bed.*

You're not going to sleep in that green thing, surely? (*Indicating the scrunchie.*)

MANDY. Oh Mummy.

MUM. All right. Night night, poppet. (*She kisses her.*)

MANDY. Night night.

MUM *exits.*

Oh Gertrude, I love my scrunchie but I wish Tanya hadn't stolen it. I saw her take it from the ice-cream shop in the park. I'm sure Mummy knows. Now she'll think I'm a thief too.

MANDY *gets into bed and tosses and turns. Music. Dream sequence.*

ANNOUNCER. Welcome to the Continental Hotel and the London Fashion show, starring top model . . . Miranda Rainbow!

MANDY *strikes a pose, then exits.* KIM *and* ARTHUR *enter as models and go through a short dance routine, then* MANDY *enters in her first green model's outfit.*

And here she comes. Isn't she gorgeous!

MANDY *joins* KIM *and* ARTHUR *and they all dance.*

Miranda is wearing a glamorous green cocktail dress with a matching scrunchie, this season's smartest accessory. Thank you, Miranda.

MANDY *blows kisses and exits to change.* KIM *and* ARTHUR *have another short dance sequence. Then* MANDY *enters in her next outfit, with a bigger scrunchie on her head.*

And now Miranda is wearing another green outfit with an even bigger scrunchie. Isn't it gorgeous! And so green!

MANDY *parades again, then exits to change into her last outfit.* KIM *and* ARTHUR *do a short dance routine. Then* MANDY *enters, wearing another green dress and an enormous scrunchie which is so heavy she can hardly walk.*

And now Miranda's wearing yet another green outfit, this time with an enormous scrunchie. Oh dear, she looks a bit like a, a . . . cabbage? I wonder where she got that hideous outfit?

KIM *suddenly approaches and pulls off* MANDY*'s dress and scrunchie.* MANDY *clutches at herself in embarrassment.*

KIM *and* ARTHUR *point at her accusingly.*

KIM/ARTHUR (*exiting*). Thief, thief, thief!

MANDY *gets back into bed, muttering 'I'm not a thief, I'm not.' Music fades.* MUM *enters.*

MANDY. I'm not, I'm not a thief. I'm not. (*Wakes up.*)

MUM. Whatever's the matter, darling?

MANDY. I – I had a horrible dream. (*She wipes her face on the sheet.*)

MUM. Hey, don't wipe your face on the sheet! Let's find you a hankie, poor little moppet. What was this horrid dream about, eh?

MANDY. I can't remember. But it was so scary.

MUM. There. Mummy's here now.

DAD *enters with a breakfast tray, places it on the table and sits.*

You and your nightmares. Poor old Mandy. Come and have some breakfast.

MANDY *exits and puts on her school clothes whilst* MUM *tidies the bed then moves to the table.*

DAD. Is she all right?

MUM. Yes, it was just a bad dream, but she seems very disturbed at the moment and I'm not too sure about this friendship with Tanya. Mandy's seeing such a lot of her. I think she might be a bad influence.

DAD. What do you mean?

MUM. Well, she's starting to act really cheeky at times. All that business after school yesterday . . . I hate the idea of her going to the park with Tanya. Nowhere's safe nowadays.

DAD. I think Tanya can look after herself – and Mandy. Have some toast.

MANDY *enters with a hairbrush, bands and school bag. She gives* MUM *the brush and one band. They each do a plait.*

Where's the trendy new hairstyle?

MUM. I think Mandy's seen sense. It's not really suitable. Eat something, please. I'm still not keen on them being so friendly. I've a good mind to stop Mandy seeing her altogether.

MANDY. No!

DAD. Oh, come on. The girls are good friends. It's great Mandy's having a bit of fun. And she needs a friend right now, especially after all that bullying.

MUM. Has all that stopped? Kim doesn't say nasty things to you now?

MANDY. She doesn't say anything now.

MUM. Well, you keep out of her way.

MUM *and* DAD *exit.*

The playground.

ARTHUR *enters with a chess set. He and* MANDY *play chess.*

ARTHUR. Your go.

MANDY *makes a move.*

No, *look*, if you put your queen there, I'll be able to take it with my knight. Don't you like playing chess, Mandy?

MANDY. Not really.

ARTHUR. Maybe you'll like it when you get better at it. I was kind of hoping we could play every lunchtime.

MANDY. Mmm.

ARTHUR. And if you're with me then Kim and Melanie and Sarah will keep away.

MANDY. You what?

ARTHUR. I think I've scared them off. They won't do anything if I'm here to look after you.

MANDY. It's nothing to do with you. It's because of my friend Tanya.

ARTHUR. How can it be Tanya? She's not even here. Though it often feels as if she is.

MANDY. What do you mean?

ARTHUR. Well, you keep yapping about her. 'My friend Tanya said this. My friend Tanya said that.' On and on. And it isn't even as if she ever says anything interesting. It's all make-up and clothes and what-the-stars-say rubbish.

MANDY. Are you saying my friend Tanya talks rubbish?

ARTHUR. I don't know, I've never talked to her. But you talk rubbish, when you babble on about her.

MANDY. Well, you can play your silly game by yourself.

MANDY *slams down a chess piece.*

ARTHUR. All right then, I will.

ARTHUR *collects the chess pieces and exits.*

The girls' toilets.

Music. KIM *and* MELANIE *enter.* MANDY *enters and sees them. She exits rapidly into a toilet cubicle. Music fades.*

KIM. There's that girl we don't speak to. We don't even say her name, do we?

MELANIE. That's right. It's a stupid name anyway.

KIM. But she's got a new friend now. A friend who thinks she's 'it'. Well, she's 'it', all right. If 'it' equals – (*Calling off.*) Filthy Slag.

MANDY (*off*). Don't you dare call Tanya a slag!

KIM. Did you see the colour of the Filthy Slag's hair? Bright orange. Like she's got a heap of dead goldfish sticking out of her head.

More laughter.

And those shoes! Wibble-wobble, wibble-wobble.

MELANIE. It's a wonder That Girl's Mumsie lets her go around with the (*Calling off.*) Filthy Slag.

KIM. Well, they're all Mumsies together, aren't they? The Filthy Slag had her little slagling in its pram.

MANDY (*bursting out of the loo*). You're talking rubbish! That baby isn't Tanya's. She just helps to look after it. And she's not a slag. She doesn't even go out with boys. She can't stick them. So shut up, both of you.

KIM. What's that stupid buzzing noise?

MELANIE. It's that little flea that's just come out of the toilet.

KIM. She's a dirty little flea – didn't even pull the chain.

They hold their noses and exit giggling.

The department store.

Music. MUM *enters and looks at a rail of girlie frocks. She holds one against* MANDY.

MANDY. No way!

MUM (*she gets another one*). Well, this one's lovely.

MANDY. It's disgusting.

MUM (*puts it back and gets another one*). Now this one really suits you.

MANDY. It's a silly baby frock.

MUM. But you look lovely, darling. We could get you pink and white ribbons to match.

MANDY. Yuck!

MUM. Mandy! How many times do I have to tell you? You're the one who's acting like a silly baby. Well, all right. If you don't like the pink one which one did you like?

MANDY. I don't want a frock at all. No one wears them.

MUM. I see. So everyone goes around in their vest and knickers?

MANDY. No. Girls wear . . . jeans and combats.

MUM. Yes, well, I don't think you suit that kind of style.

MANDY. But I want to look like the others. That's why they keep picking on me. Because I'm different.

MUM. Well, I'll buy you some shorts. And you really do need a new swimming costume.

MANDY. I want a bikini.

MUM. A bikini! Honestly, Mandy, you're as straight up and down as an ironing board!

MUM *collects her shopping bag and they journey home.*
Home.

TANYA *enters. Music fades.*

MANDY. Tanya! (*They 'high five'.*)

TANYA. I've been waiting for you. Hey, what's in the bags? Have you been getting presents, you lucky thing!

MANDY. Just shorts and a swimming costume.

TANYA. Let's see.

She grabs the bag, looks at some shorts then a swimming costume.

Oh, I like the little rabbits. Can you swim, then?

MUM (*putting the clothes back in the bag*). Oh yes, she goes swimming with her daddy every Sunday. Come on, Mandy, indoors. Teatime.

TANYA. Did your dad teach you to swim? Will he teach me? Can I come on Sunday too?

MUM *and* MANDY *freeze.* TANYA *exits.* DAD *enters.*

DAD. Of course she can come along too.

MUM *and* MANDY *unfreeze.* MANDY *whoops with delight.*

MUM. Now calm down. Let Daddy change his clothes and get comfy before you start pestering him. We'll discuss swimming later on.

MANDY. There's nothing to discuss. Daddy said *yes*. Hurrah!

MANDY *grabs the shopping bag and exits.*

MUM. I know she's taken a shine to Tanya – but I'm worried about that girl. I've been talking to Mrs Williams and she comes from a really *dreadful* background.

DAD. Poor kid. Sounds as if she's had a tough time. So shouldn't we be extra kind to her? She seems surprisingly nice, considering – and very fond of Mandy. So where's the harm? Have you ever thought Mandy might be a *good* influence on Tanya?

DAD *and* MUM *exit.*

The swimming pool.

MANDY *and* TANYA *enter.*

MANDY (*calling off*). See you in a bit, Dad.

DAD (*off*). All right girls, don't be long.

MANDY. Come on, it's this way. The changing rooms are over here.

TANYA. I'm not sure.

MANDY. Have you got your swimming costume?

TANYA. Pat's given me this horrible thing. (*Shows* MANDY *her costume.*) It's full of holes.

MANDY. You'll look fine.

TANYA. I'm not sure this is such a good idea, I can't even swim.

MANDY. It doesn't matter, we'll just bounce around.

TANYA. Like the bouncy family.

MANDY. I wish we were a proper family. I'd give anything to have you as my sister.

TANYA. Yeah, you're like my little sister now. We'll always stay together and no one'll ever split us up, right?

MANDY. Right!

Music. MANDY, TANYA *and* DAD *swim, with great whooping and much joyful water splashing.*

End of Act One.

ACT TWO

Scene Six
INDIGO

The shopping centre.

Music. MANDY *and* TANYA *enter in summer holiday clothes.*
TANYA *casually shoplifts various items. The two girls become*
separated. KIM *enters and threatens* MANDY *but* TANYA
arrives and rescues her. KIM *exits.* TANYA *steals a final item*
then she and MANDY *exit. Music fades.*

Home.

DAD, MUM *and* MANDY *enter.*

MUM. But you always go there. You break up in a few days
and I have to go to work –

MANDY. But I can't go to Melanie's any more.

MUM. Well, you'll have to go somewhere, it's the summer
holidays. Have those girls started bullying you again?

MANDY. No. Well, not really. But there's no way I can go to
Melanie's. She hates me. And I hate her.

MUM. Can't you be friends again?

MANDY. No way!!

DAD. She doesn't *want* to be friends. And I don't blame her.
Melanie's been horrible to her!

MUM. What alternative is there? She's not old enough to be
left on her own and she's *too* old for a childminder. What on
earth are we going to do?

DAD. It's obvious!

MUM. I should give in my notice?

DAD. No! Have a word with Mrs Williams. I'm sure she'd be
happy to keep an eye on Mandy. Then she and Tanya could
keep each other company. (*He exits.*)

MANDY (*shouts*). Oh yes! *Yes!* YES! Oh, Mummy, how wonderful!

MUM. Hey, hey, calm down. Now, listen to me. I want you to behave if you go to Mrs Williams. I'm not having you running wild with Tanya. There are going to be lots of rules, right?

MANDY (*kneeling in front of her mother*). To hear is to obey, O Great Mother.

MUM *exits.*

TANYA*'s bedroom.*

Music. TANYA *enters in a sparkly violet top.* MANDY *enters and they dance. Music fades.*

It's great here, it's so much better than Melanie's.

TANYA. Yeah, we have a laugh, don't we?

MANDY. I like your sparkly violet top. It's fantastic.

TANYA. It's my best 'Love Tanyanita' top for when I'm a rock star. Do you think I'll ever make it as a rock star, Mandy?

MANDY. Yeah.

TANYA. A long time ago, Love Tanyanita and Miranda Rainbow were really poor. They even had to share the same sleeping bag. Then they made a hit album and made more money than Madonna and they travelled the world in a white stretch limousine.

MANDY. You're so good at making up stories, you should write them down.

TANYA. Yeah, right. So, which shops shall we go to today?

MANDY. Whatever you like. Or we could just stay here? You're so lucky. Mrs Williams never nags you like my mum.

TANYA. Well, that's because she's my foster mum. She doesn't really care about me. Your mum nags because she's absolutely dotty about you, anyone can see that. And your dad loves you to bits.

MANDY. What about your dad?

TANYA. Him! Haven't seen him for donkey's years. Don't
want to.

MANDY. I'm sorry.

TANYA. What for?

MANDY. I didn't mean to upset you. About your dad.

TANYA. I don't give a toss about him. Or my mum, or my
brothers. They've been adopted and they're doing great. It's
just Carmel . . .

MANDY. Won't they let you see her?

TANYA. We had this supervised visit at Easter but she got all
shy – her foster mum was there and . . . Look, shut up,
Mandy. I don't want to talk about it, OK?

MANDY. OK.

TANYA. Come on, let's go into town.

MANDY. But my mum'll be here soon.

TANYA. Don't be daft. Your mum doesn't come till half one.
Why don't you ever want to go shopping any more? (*She
puts on a hooded top.*)

MANDY. You know why.

TANYA. Why?

MANDY. Because. I don't like it when you . . .

TANYA. When I what?

MANDY. You know.

TANYA. No. So *tell* me.

MANDY. When you . . . take things.

TANYA. But I always nick something for you.

MANDY. Yes, but . . . I wish you wouldn't. I get so scared.

TANYA. Look, it's OK. I know what I'm doing. I won't get
caught, honest. I never do.

MANDY. But . . . it's wrong.

TANYA. *What?* Oh, give me a break.

MANDY. It's stealing.

TANYA. I know it's stealing. But they won't miss it. How else
am I going to get all the stuff I need, eh? Pat isn't exactly
generous with the pocket money though she gets paid a
fortune for looking after me. It's OK for you, Miss Goody-
Goody. You get heaps bought for you.

MANDY. I know, I'm sorry. Don't get mad with me. OK.
We'll go shopping.

TANYA. No, I've gone off the whole idea. You've spoilt it. I
used to get things for Carmel and she thought it was great.
We used to have really good fun together. But you're no fun
at all. (*She throws herself on the bed.*)

MANDY. Tanya, Tanya, please. Will you make friends?

TANYA. We're always friends, you daft banana. Look, if it
really bothers you, I won't nick any more stuff for you, OK?

MANDY. Oh, really?

TANYA. But I'm not saying I won't nick any more for *me*. You
still want to be friends?

MANDY. You're my best friend in the whole world.

TANYA. Come on then, let's go into town and cheer ourselves
up.

The shopping centre.

Music. Various SHOPPERS *enter.*

Look, a wishing well. (*She fishes out some coins.*) Look at
all these pennies. Come on, we can make loads of wishes.

She throws the coins back in and wishes.

Your turn.

MANDY *throws a coin in. Everyone freezes.*

MANDY. I wish Tanya will be my friend for ever.

Everyone unfreezes and continues shopping.

What did you wish for?

TANYA. If I tell, then it won't come true, will it? Come on,
I know where we can go. Hey look, there's another Kurt
Cobain T-shirt. It's lovely, isn't it? I'll see if Pat'll buy it.
I need new clothes for the summer.

MANDY. I've got some savings. I could buy it for you as a present.

TANYA. Thanks. That's really sweet, but you keep your money. Come on, let's go up in the lift!

MANDY and TANYA enter and exit a lift. Music.

Indigo shop.

A SHOP ASSISTANT enters.

MANDY and TANYA enter the shop.

Indigo, hey, this looks cool. In we go! (TANYA *picks up a jumper.*) Oh, these are gorgeous. (*She puts her arms in it.*)

MANDY. I could get you that instead of the T-shirt.

TANYA *shows her the price.*

Eighty-five pounds! I can't afford that.

TANYA. No one can. (*She looks across at the* SHOP ASSISTANT.) Honestly, look at that guy checking me out.

MANDY. Maybe you're not supposed to try things on.

TANYA. How can you tell what they look like if you don't try them on? Shall I get him to open the jewellery case?

MANDY. No!

TANYA. He's still staring at me.

MANDY. I thought you hated boys.

TANYA. I do. But I can't help it if they fancy me.

She walks over to some cowboy boots.

MANDY. Come on. We ought to be getting back.

TANYA. We've got bags of time and I want to try on these cowboy boots. (*She tries on a boot.*) Wicked, eh?

The SHOP ASSISTANT *approaches.*

Oh, oh! Can you get us the other boot?

SHOP ASSISTANT. No, I can't. And you can take that one off too. You kids have been hanging about here long enough. Take it off.

TANYA is humiliated. She tries to take off the boot and nearly falls over.

Look, you deaf or something? Stop messing about. You shouldn't try on boots with bare feet. It's, well, unhygienic.

The SHOP ASSISTANT *takes the boot, sniffs inside it, then returns it to the stand. TANYA puts on her shoe. On leaving the shop, she steals the jumper, stuffs it up her front, then runs. A shop alarm sounds. MANDY hesitates. TANYA returns to the shop and grabs her.*

TANYA. Mandy! Run! Run!

Music. They run out of the shop.

SHOP ASSISTANT. Oi, get back 'ere! (*He exits.*)

Scene Seven
VIOLET

The shopping centre.

MANDY *and* TANYA *travel up and off an escalator then down in the lift. The* SECURITY GUARD *enters. As the lift doors open and they exit, they are caught.*

SECURITY GUARD. Come on now, stop struggling. Don't make things worse for yourself.

TANYA. Let her go, you pig! It's got nothing to do with her. She's underage.

SECURITY GUARD. Then what are you doing involving her in shoplifting, eh?

TANYA. Who says we've been shoplifting? She isn't even *with* me. Let her go home to her mum.

SECURITY GUARD. You'll get to see your mums after the police have got here.

TANYA. I'll get to see my mum, will I? Well, that'll be a surprise.

They return to Indigo. The SHOP ASSISTANT *enters.*

SHOP ASSISTANT. Yeah, that's them. Stupid kids.

TANYA. You're the one who's the stupid poser. We were only trying on the boots. We haven't nicked *anything*.

SECURITY GUARD. He says you took one of their blue sweaters.

TANYA. Then he's a liar.

The SECURITY GUARD *removes the jumper from under* TANYA'*s top.*

SECURITY GUARD. Who's the liar?

TANYA (*to* GUARD). You planted it on me. Didn't she, Mandy? She shoved it at me to frame me.

SECURITY GUARD. You're a right tough little cookie, aren't you? I bet when the police arrive we'll find you've got a lot of previous.

MANDY. The police!

POLICEMAN *and* POLICEWOMAN *enter.*

POLICEMAN. Hey, hey! Do I really look so fierce? So who's this little shrinking violet, eh?

POLICEWOMAN. Give over, you're frightening her. What's your name, love?

MANDY. Mandy.

TANYA. She's nothing to do with this. She's just a kid who tagged after me. Let her go. Couldn't you let us both go, please?

SECURITY GUARD. She's a great little actress.

POLICEWOMAN. As both the girls are so young and your property has been recovered, do you still want to go ahead and prosecute, sir?

They all look at the SHOP ASSISTANT.

SHOP ASSISTANT. It's Indigo policy. Shoplifters are always prosecuted. Half the time it's kids like these two. They need to be taught a lesson.

POLICEMAN. In that case, sir, you'd better come with us to the station and make a full statement.

TANYA. But she's not a thief.

POLICEMAN. I'm afraid we've got reasonable grounds to think you are though, young lady. So I'm going to have to arrest you.

He cautions TANYA.

MANDY. We're not really being arrested!

POLICEWOMAN. Not you, love. But you'd need to come to the police station and tell us exactly what happened, then we'll get your mum to take you home, OK?

MANDY. But you're arresting Tanya?

POLICEWOMAN. I'm afraid so. Come on.

The SHOP ASSISTANT *exits.*

The police station.

Musical bridge. The POLICEWOMAN *exits.*

TANYA. Oh hello, the Custody Suite.

MANDY *and* TANYA *sit down next to each other. The* SERGEANT *enters.*

SERGEANT. Sit further apart, girls. Now I'm Sergeant Stockton. I want you to tell me your names and addresses then I can give your parents a ring.

TANYA. Oh, what's your mum going to say, Mandy? She'll kill me.

SERGEANT. What about your own mum?

TANYA. Haven't got one. Haven't got a dad now either. He's not considered a fit parent. So you want my appropriate adult, yeah?

SERGEANT. That's the ticket. Bet you could fill in this form quicker than me. So who's it to be?

TANYA. You'd better phone Mrs Williams, my foster mum. She'll be going spare anyway. Now look, Sergeant, I've got to make something clear. I'm going to be absolutely honest.

SERGEANT. That's right. Make my day.

TANYA. I'm serious, she's just the kid over the road. She hangs around after me. But I swear, she's never nicked a thing. She's only here because of me. So you'll let her go, won't you? You won't even caution her?

SERGEANT. It's OK. She just needed to be taken to a place of safety. But she can go as soon as her mum comes.

MANDY. What about Tanya? Will she be able to go home too?

SERGEANT. Eventually.

MANDY. What does that mean?

Music. TANYA *and* SERGEANT *exit.*

MANDY*'s home.*

MUM *and* DAD *enter. Music fades.*

MUM. I can't believe this is happening. I told you over and over again that I didn't want Mandy mixed up with that girl. But you wouldn't listen to me. You thought you knew best. And now look what's happened!

DAD. All right, all right. There's no need to rub it in. I didn't dream it would come to this. I always thought Mandy had enough sense to stick to what she knew was right. If you didn't *baby* her quite so much then maybe she'd be able to stand up for herself better.

MUM. We're terribly upset and disappointed – but we do realise it wasn't all your fault, darling.

DAD. Come on, Polly Pigtails. It's over now.

MANDY. But what about Tanya?

MUM. Never mind about Tanya!

DAD. You'll find a new friend soon.

MANDY. But Tanya's my best friend! She won't go shoplifting ever again. She promised. And she hated getting me into trouble. She could have run away and left me but she didn't. So what's going to happen? Has she got to go to court?

MUM (*nods*). Thank goodness you're not involved.

DAD. I thought they'd just caution her.

MUM. Apparently she's had lots of cautions already. They're going to make a full case history. It's likely to take weeks.

MANDY. So she'll be here for weeks?

MUM. No, dear, Tanya's going to a children's home. Mrs Williams says she can't cope and I can see her point.

DAD. She's just washing her hands of Tanya?

MUM. What else can she do?

MANDY. If I'd stolen that jumper would you get rid of me?

MUM. Don't be silly, Mandy.

MANDY. But *would* you?

MUM. No, of course not. You know we wouldn't. We love you and we'll go on loving you no matter what you do.

DAD. But no one loves poor old Tanya.

MANDY. I do! And Mum didn't even want us to be friends, did you?

MUM. Now, now. All right, I didn't think it was very sensible and I was proved right, but there's no need to look at me like that. I didn't have anything against Tanya personally. It's just that she wasn't the right age for you, and she didn't come from the right kind of background.

MANDY. Melanie's the right age, the right background, the right sort of friend for me. And she was really mean and ganged up with Kim and Sarah. They're horrible to me. Tanya was always great.

DAD. That's a good point.

MUM. It's not as simple as that. But I wish I'd tried a bit harder.

MANDY. It's easy to say that now.

DAD. When is she leaving?

MUM. Well, right now. It does seem a bit . . . but I suppose there's no point dragging things out.

MANDY. *Now?* I've got to say goodbye.

MUM. No, you're not going anywhere near her.

DAD. Maybe it's not such a good idea.

MANDY. I've got to. And you can't stop me.

*MANDY exits. MUM and DAD look at each other wearily
then exit.*

*TANYA's bedroom. TANYA packs her belongings into a
plastic carrier bag, then she strips the bed. MANDY enters
with large set of rainbow felt-tip pens.*

Hi Tanya.

TANYA. Hi Mandy.

MANDY. You're going?

TANYA. Yeah. Pat's booting me out. I was only here for a
while anyway. I'm going to this new children's home. It'll
be a dump. They all are. Dumping grounds for kids nobody
wants.

MANDY. I want you, Tanya! (*She hugs her.*)

TANYA. Don't worry, I'll write. (*She sees the pens.*) What did
you bring them over for anyway? It's not like we've got
time to do any colouring.

MANDY. They're for you. A goodbye present.

TANYA. All of them?

MANDY. Well, one or two wouldn't be much good.

TANYA. You can't give me your rainbow felt-tips. What'll
your mum say?

MANDY. It's not up her. They're mine, and I want you to have
them.

TANYA. No one's ever given me such a lovely present. Thank
you so much. I'd better find a present for you.

Music. She hunts in her bag and finds her violet sparkly top.

Here! You have it.

MANDY. I can't. It's your special top.

TANYA. That's why I want you to have it. My best thing for
my best friend. Bye Mandy.

MANDY. Bye Tanya.

TANYA *starts to exits with her bag and the pens, then turns. She and* MANDY *do their special handshake, then she exits.*

Scene Eight
RAINBOW

MANDY*'s bedroom.*

MANDY *sits on her bed and holds up* TANYA*'s top against herself. She puts it on, then gets out a mirror with delight, but she is horrified at her image. She pulls off the top and knocks her glasses to the floor. She gropes for them as* MUM *enters.*

MUM. Mandy?

MANDY (*finding glasses*). Oh no!

MUM. What's the matter?

MANDY. I've broken my glasses again.

MUM. Well, we'll see if Daddy can fix them. But we'll get you a new pair soon.

MANDY. Really grown-up fashionable glasses?

MUM. Yes. So long as they're not too expensive.

MANDY. And can I have my hair cut instead of these stupid plaits?

MUM. I'm not so sure about that. If it's really important then maybe. It is your hair after all. But I'm telling you one thing, you're not wearing that – (*Indicating* TANYA*'s top.*) outdoors.

MANDY. It doesn't fit anyway. It looked lovely on Tanya.

MUM. Well . . .

MANDY. She said she'd write, but she hates writing, so I don't think she will.

MUM. I know you miss her, darling, and I understand. But believe me, you'll make some other friends soon. You need to get out more. Tell you what, they're doing some story-writing sessions at the library. Why don't you do that?

MANDY. No, Mummy! I don't *want* to. I don't want to do anything.

Music. MUM *tries to cheer up* MANDY. DAD *enters carrying a case with new rainbow glasses inside and a bag of writing things. He presents the glasses to* MANDY *who is delighted. She tries them on and* MUM *holds a mirror for her to see.* MUM *exits.*

The library.

A LIBRARIAN *enters pushing a book trolley.* ARTHUR *enters and sits.* DAD *gives* MANDY *a hug.*

Music fades.

LIBRARIAN. Mr White, is it?

DAD. That's right. And this is Mandy.

DAD *waits as* MANDY *sits then he exits. Music fades.*

LIBRARIAN. Welcome to the library, Mandy. Maybe you'd like to sit with Sarah and Julie and work on their Woodland Bunny story?

MANDY. No, thanks. I don't really want to write about rabbits. I'll make up my own.

LIBRARIAN. What are you writing today, Arthur?

ARTHUR. It's nothing, just . . . No, honestly.

LIBRARIAN. Don't be daft. Let's see.

ARTHUR *hands her his writing book. She reads.*

The Knight Who Wouldn't Fight. That's sounds interesting.

We hear children's voices.

ZAP. *The Knight Who Wouldn't Fight*!

POW. What a dumb wimpy title.

ZAP. By a dumb wimpy boy.

POW. Dumb, wimpy, nitty-Knighty Arthur.

LIBRARIAN. Now then, you two, stop being so silly. Come over here and sit with me. Chop, chop. Don't take any notice of them, Arthur.

LIBRARIAN *exits.* MANDY *crosses to* ARTHUR.

MANDY. Can I see what you've written? I can see really well
with my new rainbow glasses. I bet those two haven't even
heard of King Arthur. They're still at the *Tweenies* stage.
Let's have a look.

ARTHUR. Here.

MANDY *looks at the story.*

MANDY. It's good. I tell you what, let's do a story together,
about a beautiful medieval witch, Mandiana the Magic and
an all-powerful wizard called Dark Art! Get it? Art for
Arthur!

Music.

ARTHUR. Yeah, that'll be fabulous. We should make our own
costumes.

He gets a ruler out of his bag.

Look, this can be a wand.

*He 'magics' the bag, takes out a spare T-shirt and puts it on
his head.*

I know, and this can be my cape. Look, quick, see what you
got?

MANDY (*looks in her bag and takes out a cardigan. Ties it
round her shoulders*). This is my cloak and this is my bag
of explosions. Make a cauldron, Arthur.

ARTHUR. Oh yeah, 'cos they have them then, don't they?

He spins the chair as a cauldron.

MANDY. Let's dance around it.

They do so.

Let's do a special sign.

ARTHUR. What, like a special move?

They improvise a special movement.

Quick, the evil spirits of Camelot are coming. They're just
around the corner. They look really savage.

MANDY. Let's make something to escape on.

ARTHUR. Yes, like a kind, flying dragon.

MANDY sits on the book trolley and ARTHUR pushes her round.

Yes, we're escaping. Dark Art and Mandiana, the greatest wizards in all of Camelot!

He exits with trolley.

MANDY. Dark Art and Mandiana!

Home.

MUM enters with a carrier bag. She sits dejectedly. MANDY is very happy and doesn't notice.

Hi Mummy. Did you get my cardigan?

MUM hands her the bag. She looks at the cardigan in it.

Yes! No rabbits! – Mummy, what's the matter? Has something happened to Tanya?

MUM. No, of course not. I've just had a little shock. I've lost my job. I'm sorry, darling. It's not the end of the world. Don't know why I'm making such a fuss.

MANDY. You'll get another job.

MUM. I'm not so sure. It was awful. I had to clear my desk and get out straightaway. I couldn't believe it was happening. My boss said it was because I was unreliable. He kept on about all the time off I'd had, what with my teeth playing up and then when I had to look after you –

MANDY. So it's my fault?

MUM. No, no! Of course not. He said I was too old-fashioned. But what he really meant was that I was too *old*.

MANDY. But you're not old, Mummy. Well, not *that* old.

MUM. Yes I am. When I look at the other mums at school, I'm old enough to be *their* mum. (*She cries into her hankie.*)

MANDY. You'll get another job, Mummy, I know you will. Don't worry, I think you're brilliant. And I'm really glad you're my mum. Shall I make you a cup of tea?

MUM. Thank you, darling, that would be lovely.

MANDY *puts her arm round* MUM *and they exit with the shopping bag.*

Classroom.

The school bell rings. KIM *enters, followed by* ARTHUR.

ARTHUR. I'm the classroom monitor this week and Mr Moseley says we've got to clear the classroom.

KIM. Well, you can do it. I'm not moving.

ARTHUR. All right then, I will.

Grand Camelot music. ARTHUR *clears everything much to* KIM's *annoyance. Music ends.*

SARAH, MELANIE *and* MANDY *enter and sit gossiping.*

Hey, Mandy. Come and sit next to me.

MANDY. I can't. You're a boy.

ARTHUR. Brilliant deduction. So what?

MANDY *sits next to* ARTHUR. *The others make stupid remarks.*

Nutters.

MANDY. Nutters.

KIM. They're the nutty ones. Two swotty little twits, sticking together because they haven't got any other friends.

ARTHUR. Take no notice.

MANDY. I won't, 'cos it's not true. I've got Tanya, and – (*Mumbles.*) I've got you. So what do you think of our new teacher?

ARTHUR. I really like him.

MANDY. So do I. I like his cardigan.

ARTHUR. I've had fun this week. But what's with this Circle Time thing we have to do? Maybe we'll draw circles with protractors.

MANDY. What, make patterns? I like doing that. Then we can colour them in.

MR MOSELEY *enters.*

MR MOSELEY. Good afternoon, children.

CLASS. Good afternoon, Mr Moseley.

MR MOSELEY. Well done, you've made a circle. Oh, come on, you three. You can't work all squashed up like that. Kim, come and sit on the over here, please. Kim? Come and sit here, please.

KIM. No, I'll stay here. Melanie can move.

MR MOSELEY. It's not up to you. I'm the teacher and I say who sits where. Melanie and Sarah, stay where you are. Kim, move to make a circle. At once!

KIM *gets up and moves.*

Right. Now we're all sorted out and sitting comfortably, we can start our lesson. Circle Time is going to be our special time on a Friday afternoon, where we all sit round as a class and talk about all sorts of different things.

KIM. Oooh, he's going to tell us about sex.

MR MOSELEY. Not today, folks. So you can all simmer down. Circle Time is when we discuss various issues.

CHILD. What's an issue, Mr Moseley?

KIM (*pretending to sneeze*). Issue! Issue!

MR MOSELEY. An issue is something important that's on our minds at the moment. Something we want to talk about . . .

CHILD. Like *EastEnders*?

MR MOSELEY. Not exactly. But all sorts of issues are dealt with in *EastEnders*. Anyway, today, I thought we might like to talk about bullying.

Silence falls. Everyone looks at KIM.

I know it's uncomfortable to think about, but now you're in a new class, you're ready to discuss very painful grown-up topics. Now instead of all speaking out at once, if you want to talk, come in to the centre of the circle and pick up Cedric the Snail. Sarah.

SARAH *places a stone snail in the middle of the group.*

So, what do you all think we should do about bullies?

Music. The group circle round. As one of them picks up Cedric and speaks, the music stops and the rest sit and listen, then music comes in again and they circle.

CHILD. I think they should get beaten up, too.

CHILD. No one should ever talk to them ever again.

CHILD. But wouldn't we be just as horrible as them?

CHILD. So why do people bully?

Short blast of music.

CHILD. Because they think they're strong and they want to hurt other children.

CHILD. Because they're horrible like boys.

CHILD. Because they like scaring people, like the Dementors in the *Harry Potter* film.

MANDY. They like to gang up on you.

ARTHUR. And if you're not in the gang you get left out and picked on.

KIM *knocks over Cedric the Snail. The others are shocked by this.*

KIM. Sometimes they ask for it because they are stupid.

ARTHUR (*puts Cedric straight, then picks him up*). And sometimes they get bullied because they are clever. Say they come top of the class and the bully doesn't like it because they're clever too and *they* want to be top.

CHILD. So, if someone is being bullied what should you do?

Short blast of music.

CHILD. Tell someone at once.

CHILD. Tell your mum and dad.

CHILD. Tell a teacher.

MANDY. But sometimes it doesn't work.

CHILD. You got to keep on and on or it gets worse and worse.

CHILD. It makes you feel lonely.

ARTHUR. You try and ignore them, but they won't leave you alone.

CHILD. That's like my mum's dog, and it never leaves you alone and it bites all the other dogs, on their bum!

CHILD. Or I went to the zoo and there were all these big monkeys and they were really bullying the little monkeys but all the big monkeys had big red bottoms!

They all laugh, except KIM.

CHILD (*at KIM*). Bullies have smelly red bottoms!

The school bell rings.

MR MOSELEY. Thank you everyone, some wonderful ideas there. We'll continue this next week in our next Circle Time. But please make sure that you think about what we've discussed today. OK? Well done.

The CHILDREN wish MR MOSELEY goodbye and exit.

Are you all right, Kim?

KIM. Yeah.

She exits. MR MOSELEY exits.

Bus stop.

Music. There is a rumble of thunder. ARTHUR enters. MELANIE and SARAH enter and talk together. KIM enters.

Why didn't you wait for me?

The girls don't answer. KIM stands on her own. MANDY enters. KIM threatens her. MANDY faces up to KIM. There is a crash of thunder. ARTHUR goes to MANDY.

ARTHUR. Over here, Mandy.

He and MANDY leave KIM. It starts to rain. All, except KIM, exit as the bus arrives. The bus drives away.

KIM. Hey, wait for me! (*KIM exits.*)

Home.

DAD enters. MANDY enters, wet from the rain.

MANDY. Hi Daddy.

DAD. Hi poppet.

MANDY. Why are you home so early? And where's Mummy?

DAD. Good news. I'm home early because . . . Guess what? Your mum's gone for an interview for a new job, and she's got it! And . . . look what came in the post for you this morning. (*He hands her a postcard.*)

MANDY. I don't believe it. A postcard from Tanya!

DAD exits as MANDY goes to her bedroom and sits on her bed.

TANYA'S VOICE. 'Hi Mandy. I said I'd write. The juvenile court was a doddle. I just got a supervision order. Great, eh? And I think I'm getting a new foster mum, so things are looking up. See you, best friend. Lots of love, Tanya. Kiss kiss.'

MANDY. 'Dear Tanya, Glad you're well. I am well too. I am in a new class and I have new glasses. I'm not on my own any more. I sit next to Arthur and it's OK. Still, I miss you tons. But you haven't put an address, so I hope you come back and see me. If you don't, I will look for you when I'm older. Lots of love, Mandy – See you, best friend, somewhere . . . '

Music. A rainbow appears with TANYA at the top, looking down at MANDY. Music fades.

Blackout.

The End.